I0648177

Sabine Baring-Gould

Nazareth and Capernaum

Ten lectures on the beginning of our Lord's ministry

Sabine Baring-Gould

Nazareth and Capernaum
Ten lectures on the beginning of our Lord's ministry

ISBN/EAN: 9783337257774

Printed in Europe, USA, Canada, Australia, Japan

Cover: Foto ©Lupo / pixelio.de

More available books at **www.hansebooks.com**

Nazareth and Capernaum.

Nazareth and Capernaum.

TEN LECTURES

ON THE

BEGINNING OF OUR LORD'S MINISTRY.

BY

REV. S. BARING GOULD, M.A.,

authorAUTHOR OF "THE NATIVITY," "THE TRIALS OF JESUS," "THE PASSION,"
"THE SEVEN LAST WORDS," ETC.

London:

SKEFFINGTON AND SON, 163, PICCADILLY.

—

1886.

Contents.

Nazareth and Capernaum.

I.

The Wilderness.*

S. MATTHEW IV. 1.

" Then was Jesus led up of the Spirit into the wilderness to be tempted of the devil."

IT is certainly a fact full of significance, that the first impulse of the Divine Spirit after having descended on Christ should be to drive Him into seclusion. The Baptism had been attended with marvellous signs—the opening of Heaven, the visible descent of the Spirit, and the voice proclaiming the Sonship of Christ. This was a manifestation of Christ to the people, before He began His mission ; a proclamation to all those who came to Jordan to the baptism of Repentance, that He was come, of Whom the prophets had spoken, and to Whom John the Baptist was the herald.

Then—when He had thus been declared to be the expected of Israel—then the Spirit leads Him away from the society of men to spend forty days and nights in prayer and fasting in the wilderness. It was almost certainly the

---

* Suitable for the First Sunday in Lent.

A

same after the conversion of S. Paul. He went into Arabia, without conferring "with flesh and blood" (Gal. i. 16, 17), before he began to exercise his ministry.

Surely we may learn from this that the Divine Spirit urges to humility and withdrawal from the society of men—and how different is this from the blustering and obtrusive self-laudation which we sometimes see in those who regard themselves as converted characters. The Spirit declared Christ to be the Son of God, in Whom the Father was well pleased, and at—once He fled to the desert and hid Himself. On another occasion He performed a great miracle of feeding many thousands, and that performed, He retired into a mountain apart to pray.

We live in a busy time, when action alone is regarded, and we lightly esteem whatever work does not make display. We must advertise ourselves, proclaim our successes, puff our work, and regard success as the seal of Divine favour. Yet the silent forty days and nights of prayer and fasting, and struggle with the tempter, produced no apparent results, effected nothing positive that we can see, yet the Lord began His ministry with this, as though this were essential to His success. A time of retirement from business, of gathering in of the thoughts from the routine of work, of abstraction from vulgar cares, is necessary for all; and without it, advancement in the spiritual life, and success in the ministerial work of saving or shepherding souls is not to be expected. The disciples of Jesus were unable to cast out devils, because they had not prepared for the attempt in the same way as Christ. "This goeth not out," said our Lord, "but by prayer and fasting." (S. Matt. xvii. 21.)

It has been said that Christ by His example sanctioned the eremitical life, the retirement into the deserts of the old hermits, to spend their lives in contemplation. To some extent only is this true. Christ sanctioned retirement, but He made retirement from the world preparatory to active mission work in the world. Where the old hermits misread His teaching was in this, that they retired to the deserts and did not leave the deserts again, they made that a *cul-de-sac* which should have been a passage.

The example of our Lord seems to us in this age of high pressure to be of special importance. We look too much to the amount of work done, rather than to the quality of the work. This is the case in every branch of life, in every industry, in every profession; and it cannot be denied that in the present day the hurry of life is so great that men have not the patience to study and to appreciate good work; so long as it has a specious appearance of being good, it is sufficient. But in spiritual work, we must consider that the eye of God is on us, and that we are labouring for Him, not for men, and, by His retirement for prayer and fasting into the solitude of the desert, Christ puts into our hands the key to the door of all thorough and efficacious work in the spiritual sphere,— it must be well considered, well prayed over, and well prepared for.

Every plant has its hidden life that precedes its visible and manifested life ; the seed, or bulb, or tuber spends a time in accumulating to itself vital force or energy, during which period it appears to be dormant.   Then, when it has taken the requisite time, it begins to grow, it throws up its leaves and flowers.   The leaves and flowers are no spontaneous development out of the root, they have been long prepared for in the hidden life and apparent sleep of the seed or root underground.   All life is initiated by a hidden period of incubation.   And all healthy human activity has also its still, unperceived phase of existence.   Christ shows us that it is the same in the spiritual life.   The forty days and nights —I may say the whole of the hidden life at Nazareth—was the seed germinating, and the three years' ministry was the manifestation of the life.

The wilderness into which our Blessed Lord retired lies to the east of the Dead Sea, the most barren district of Palestine, where deeply cleft ravines and naked crags present a picture of Nature bereft of life.   The rocks are of volcanic origin, black, and there are beds of lava.   The lower ravine of the Cedron not inappropriately bears the name of the Vale of Fire.   This barren waste was a figure of the world into which Christ had come, bare of all the fruits of righteousness, dry of all waters of comfort, destitute of green pastures, possessed as an habitation by men with the passions of wild beasts, haunted by evil spirits. Into this desert the Scape Goat was annually driven, there, as the Jews believed, to be torn to pieces by devils. Into this desert the Lamb of God enters, that He may combat and break the power of Satan.

The children of Israel, after having traversed the Red Sea, and been baptized under Moses in that sea, as the Apostle says, were disciplined in the wilderness for forty years, to prepare them to take the Land of Promise into possession, and now the Son of Israel, after having been baptized in Jordan, retires into the wilderness to prepare by self-discipline for taking to Himself the Kingdom.

Solitude is the mother of great thoughts and resolutions. There. on the heights of Abarim, Christ could look down on the Dead Sea, into which the sweet waters of Jordan incessantly flowed, yet which they never sweetened. So had the stream of life which God had created, full of good, and health, and sweetness, run down into a Sea of Death, and it seemed impossible that the corruption of life in the world could be cured. But now, a new well of water,—the Water of Life was to be opened, a new stream poured forth, and the prophecy of Ezekiel be fulfilled, "These waters issue out towards the east country, and go down into the desert, and go into the sea, and the waters shall be healed. And it shall come to pass, that every thing that liveth, which

moveth, whithersoever the rivers shall come, shall live—
everything shall live whither the river cometh." (Ezek.
xlvii. 8, 9.)

It may be doubted whether any other scene on earth
can surpass the desert of Engedi for rousing in the mind
thoughts of death and judgment. This valley, now converted
to a desert, was once a well-watered and populous plain,
in which stood five cities full of life, and happiness, and
activity. Lot chose this broad valley as his share, because
of its fertility, and now it is all desolation—ashes, dust, and
flinty rock. The ruin of one district, brought about by the
spirit of fleshly lust. The transformation of the garden into
a desert and a Dead Sea, is a figure of the ruin of the world;
of the desolation wrought, moreover, in man by the spirit of
uncleanness. There Jesus sees before Him, as in a picture,
the then condition of the world; the transformation, the
regeneration He was sent from Heaven to effect.

He begins His work with Himself. Before He goes out
on His mission to destroy the works of the Devil on men,
He proves the power of Satan on Himself; before He shews
men how the flesh is to be conquered, He tests in Himself
the power and weakness of the flesh.

Here, then, is an important lesson to all those who would
do good to others. Let them first prove themselves. You
will remember the scorn with which S. Paul addresses those
who rush to instruct, reprove, exhort others, without having

prepared for it by self-introspection. " Thou which teachest another, teachest thou not thyself? Thou that preachest a man should not steal, dost thou steal? Thou that sayest a man should not commit adultery, dost thou commit adultery? Thou that abhorrest idols, dost thou commit sacrilege? Thou that makest thy boast of the law, through breaking the law dishonourest thou God?" (Rom. ii. 21-23.)

The Lord foresaw His temptation, and He prepared for it. He shewed us, therefore, that we must be on our guard, and watch and make ready against the Evil One. He who is unprepared is likely to fall a prey to Satan, but he who has prepared his soul against temptations is secure. "Watch and pray lest ye enter into temptation," was our Lord's command to His disciples in the Garden, but it is an exhortation appropriate to all who are His disciples, and at all times. The retirement of our Lord into the wilderness, therefore, teaches us several precious lessons.

1. Humility when most favoured by God, when most abundantly illumined and blessed by His Spirit.

2. The necessity of preparation for every work done for God, if that work is to be really fruitful.

3. All missionary and ministerial work is to be begun with self.

4. Preparation is necessary against the temptations of the Evil One.

II

The Temptation.*

S. MATTHEW IV. 3.

"The tempter came to Him."

"AND when" Jesus " had fasted forty days and forty nights, He was afterward an hungred.   And when the tempter came to Him, he said, If Thou be the Son of God, command that these stones be made bread."   Or, as S. Luke says, "Command this stone that it be made bread."   "But He answered and said, It is written, Man shall not live by bread alone, but by every word that proceedeth out of the mouth of God."   As the first Adam in the Garden of Eden was tempted through his fleshly appetite, so is the second Adam tempted in the desert.   The first Adam was not hungry, he was merely attracted by the looks of the fruit of the forbidden tree, which promised to be as delicious to the palate as it was pleasant to the eye.   The second Adam had fasted for forty days and forty nights and was famished.   There was something infantile in the temptation to which the first man was subjected.   A babe tries to put everything in its mouth. A child is greedy, its ruling passion is love of sweet things

* Suitable for the First Sunday in Lent.

and fruit. Satan, in tempting our first parents, used the sort of temptation which is most likely to prevail with children. The second Adam was tried in a somewhat different way. He was not assailed with the temptation to yield to the love of sweet things, but to the craving after necessary food; and this shows us that Satan did not approach Him with that sardonic contempt and effrontery with which he encountered the first Adam.

There is nothing more beautiful than the childlike, simple character, and this the first Adam possessed; he was ignorant of evil, guileless. Satan, with that scoffing spirit with which the great German poet has portrayed him, to show his scorn of this innocent mind, tempts him with the sort of temptation which even a school-boy or a little girl of six years old would have the moral courage to resist.

But in the first temptation of our Lord there is no token of this sneering spirit. The devil recognises the gravity of the case, and he tries Christ more seriously than he tried Adam.

Jesus had been baptized. The voice from Heaven had proclaimed Him to be the Son of God. Satan appeals to this manifestation, " If Thou be the Son of God, command that these stones be made bread." But if he addresses himself somewhat differently to the task of working the fall of the second Adam, he tries the same method of insinuating a doubt. To our first parents he said, " Yea, hath God

said, ye shall not eat?" and when Eve exclaimed that God
had said, "Ye shall not eat of it, neither shall ye touch it,
lest ye die," he replied, "Ye shall not surely die." He
hinted first his doubt of God having given the command,
then his disbelief in God's threat being carried out. So now
he hints that the voice from Heaven was *Vox et præterea nihil.*

The temptation was shrewdly contrived to meet the
peculiar circumstances. In my last lecture I shewed how
that the desert and the Dead Sea, lying in the basin of the
barren hills, were a figure of the desolation brought on the
world by sin, and how that probably our Lord, from the
wilderness, looked over this picture of death, and saw in it a
figure of the scene of His moral operation. Now Satan steals
up to Him, holding out a dead stone, and asks Him to begin
His work by transforming that stone. As He is about to make
the desert fruitful, and the wilderness blossom as a rose, and
the Sea of Death become a lake of living water, let Him
begin His work symbolically, with a stone of this district.
Very probably the temptation was not to turn the piece of
black stone into white wheaten bread, but into the homely,
hard rye, black bread, which nourishes, but is no dainty.

On the way to Jericho, and, indeed, all around the Dead
Sea, are to be found in chalk beds, masses of flint, of rounded
shape, which the Arabs suppose to be the olives, apples,
melons, and other fruit of the time of Sodom and Gomorrah,
which, at the overthrow of the cities, were turned into stone.

Some of these stones have the size and shape of loaves, and it is possible that Satan took one of these rounded masses of flint, and, with his undercurrent of bitterness and scorn, offered it to Christ, supposing Him to share the popular superstition about them. If we may expand his words, they ran thus : " See this loaf-like flintstone ! No doubt it was once bread in one of the houses of Sodom, but God over-threw the wicked city, and the bread was turned into stone. Now, O Son of God—that is, if you are the Son of God—as you have come to undo the work of destruction wrought by sin, and to bring life into a world subject to death, shew your power on this stone, and turn it back into the loaf of bread which it once was."

Our Lord answered, " Man doth not live by bread alone, but by every word that proceedeth out of the mouth of God." His reply to Satan shewed that man has a double nature, a spiritual as well as a material life. Satan had assailed Him through His animal nature, His carnal needs. Christ points out to him that man has a spiritual nature as well, and spiritual needs. Moreover, He shewed Satan that He was come to work miracles not for the relief of His own necessity, but for the mitigation of the distresses and needs of His fellow men.

Satan understands at once. He is keen of intellect ; the drift of our Lord's words is quite clear to his cold, cruel intelligence, and instantly he changes the nature of his temptation, and assails Christ's spiritual nature, that nature which craved for and lived by the word of God.

The assaults of Satan are in three spheres—the sensual, the ethical, and the spiritual. Directly that he has been defeated in his attack on Christ through His physical necessities, he alters his tactics, and seeks His overthrow through an appeal to His higher, spiritual nature.

"Then the devil taketh Him up into the holy city, and setteth Him on a pinnacle of the Temple, and saith unto Him, If Thou be the Son of God, cast Thyself down : for it is written, He shall give His angels charge concerning Thee : and in their hands they shall bear Thee up, lest at any time Thou dash Thy foot against a stone."

The holy city is, of course, Jerusalem.* The pinnacle (πτερύγιον τοῦ ἱεροῦ) is properly the wing of the Temple buildings, not of the main building (τοῦ ναοῦ) itself. The pinnacle has been supposed to be the pediment of the three-storied royal hall, which Herod had erected at the southern corner of the Temple area, and which reached to the mouth of the Tyropœon, and stood high above the ravine of Cedron, where it turns into the Valley of Hinnom. Josephus thus describes it. † "It was an astonishing work of art, the like of which was nowhere else to be seen, for the valley was so

---

* The attribute " Kedoscha " (holy) is given to Jerusalem in Isaiah xlviii. 2. Jerusalem to this day is called by the natives El Kods, the Holy.

† Antiq. xv. 11, 5.

deep, that when anyone standing on the top looked down into it, he lost his head. Above this, Herod erected a portico of four storeys of pillars, of such extraordinary height, that when anyone ascended to the parapet, so as to look down from the roof on the entire depth of building and natural precipice, he stood a chance of becoming giddy before his eye reached the bottom of the abyss." The parapet here, no doubt, formed a low pediment, such as is common to the gables of Grecian temples. On the top of this pediment stood Jesus, with Satan by Him.

A great commotion, and, indeed, a riot was caused in Jerusalem, by the erection of a golden Roman eagle, on the Temple gate, as crowning the pediment, by Herod the Great, about 4 B.C. The eagle was torn down and broken in pieces by the rioters. It was a symbol both of Roman power and of Jupiter, the king of the gods. Now—perhaps in covert reference to this incident—Satan plants the Lord on the apex of the pediment of Herod's great four-storied hall, or, possibly on the entrance gate, on the very pedestal from which the golden eagle had been thrown down.

We may again expand the temptation of Satan, to give its full significance. " See ! Thou Who art—or art declared to be, the Son of God, standest now on the pediment of the Temple. When Herod, the builder of this splendid pile, set up on it the golden image of the bird that symbolized the heathen god and Roman power, the Jews pulled it down and it was dashed to pieces. Now Thou, the promised Messiah art come, Thou standest on the highest and most conspicuous point of the gable ; now then, manifest Thyself to the Jews for what Thou givest Thyself out to be. Throw Thyself down, and let them see Thou art not man only. The golden eagle was smashed when it fell, but angels will bear Thee up, and this manifestation will shew Thy people that Thou art the true Messiah, come to release them from the yoke of the Romans." Satan's temptation was now an incentive to spiritual pride. He tried to spur Christ, Who had "made Himself a little lower than the angels," by His incarnation, to shew Himself to be the Lord of the angels ; to make Himself, as man, equal with God. The apostate angels as lightning fell from Heaven, because they sought to exalt themselves to be equal with God, and now Satan tries on Christ the same temptation which had wrought his own fall, as in the first instance he tried on Christ the temptation which had effected Adam's fall. Adam fell through lust of the flesh, Satan through spiritual ambition. Now Satan having failed to bring Christ down by attacking His human nature, attacks His spiritual nature.

It is certainly remarkable that not long after, at the destruction of Jerusalem, hundreds of Jews threw themselves down from the top of the Temple, in the belief that at the last moment God would send the Messiah to deliver them and the holy city and His Temple by a miracle.

They sinned in the way in which Christ refused to sin.

That is mistrust in the ordinary grace of God, when man, either through pride or timidity, exacts of God an extraordinary manifestation of His power.

It is worthy of remark, that Satan quoted Scripture to enforce his temptation, taking a text and breaking it away from its context, "Thou shalt tread upon the lion and adder," which refers to the triumph of Christ over himself. We may learn from this to mistrust all fancy picking and choosing in Scripture of texts and doctrines. The Catholic faith is the entire circle of verities revealed by Christ to His Church. Heresy, which is the work of the devil, is the breaking away and exaggerating of one truth at the expense of others. Our Lord answered, "It is written again, Thou shalt not tempt the Lord thy God."

"Again, the devil taketh Him up into an exceeding high mountain, and sheweth Him all the kingdoms of the world, and the glory of them : and saith unto Him, All these things will I give Thee if Thou wilt fall down and worship me."

The high mountain is most probably Abarim, with its three peaks of Pisgah, Peor and Nebo. From the western point, Peor, Balaam overlooked the tents of Israel and blessed them, when brought there by Balak to curse the people. From the northernmost peak, Nebo, above Baal Maon, a complete panorama of the Dead Sea is obtained. Thence it was that the Lord God shewed Moses " All the land of Gilead, unto Dan, and all Naphtali, and the land of Ephraim, and Manasseh, and all the land of Judah, unto the utmost sea, and the south, and the plain of the valley of Jericho, the city of palm trees, unto Zoar. And the Lord said unto him, This is the land which I sware unto Abraham, unto Isaac, and unto Jacob, saying, I will give it unto thy seed : I have caused thee to see it with thine eyes, but thou shalt not go over thither." (Deut. xxxiv. 1-4.)

Here once more we notice the covert sneer in Satan's temptation. He takes Christ to the point where Moses stood to view the Promised Land which he was *not* to enter. Let us again expand the tempter's words, and give the temptation its full force and significance. " O Thou prophet of the Most High, like unto Moses, Who comest to lead the people of God out of bondage into liberty, to restore again the kingdom to Israel ! Thou wilt, may be, do what Thou undertakest. But what will be the result to *Thyself?* Wilt Thou profit in any way by it ? God gave to Moses a hard forty years in the wilderness, and instead of rewarding him with rest at the end, let him see the Promised Land from afar, even from this spot, and let him die without allowing him to set foot on it. That is how God deals with His prophets, and that is how He will deal with Thee."

And as he spake, may be the eye of the Son of Man rested on far-off Calvary, which is visible from this spot.

Then Satan went on with the contrast—" But I—I reward

my servants at once. Come, bend the knee to me, and I will give Thee glory, and power, and dominion in the present." And there rose a mirage of the desert, and in that mirage was a vision of palaces and palm trees, and glittering sheets of water, on which gay barges sailed, apparently very real, but it was only a phantom scene painted in the unwholesome vapours that rose from the Dead Sea, and from the hot bituminous desert sands and rocks. A phantom splendour over desolation and death. That was what Satan offered. And observe likewise the difference between his offers and those of God, offers which he makes quite unabashed, and emphasizes. God gives present pain and future glory— Satan gives present satisfaction and future wretchedness. Only note how he pitches on one half of each offer, and contrasts only the present, saying nothing of the future. God gives present sadness, Satan present satisfaction ; and he utters not a word about the future.

The vision was but for a moment. Satan "shewed unto Him in a moment of time all the kingdoms of the world, and the glory of them " (S. Luke iv. 5, 6) ; the desert mirage does not last long, but while it lasts it is thoroughly deceptive. So is it with the gifts of Satan; they are but for a moment, and then they vanish away, and leave dust, and ashes, and barrenness, and death behind. The devil fits his temptation nicely to his purpose. Christ is about to begin His mission, and to found His kingdom,

B

which is to be universal, to extend throughout the world. Satan shews Him how to make the kingdoms of earth His own instantaneously, by doing homage to himself. No need then for Calvary, no laborious preachings, no persecutions, no martyrdoms, no sowing in tears, no casting of the bread on the waters, and patient expectance of the result after many days. The kingdoms of the world will become the kingdoms of Christ at once, if He will conform to the world, and acknowledge the Evil One as supreme,— if He will allow the presence of evil, legislate for it, accept it, and not fight against it.

But this offer of Satan is an usurpation of power. God had said by the mouth of David, " Desire of ME, and I will give Thee the heathen for Thine inheritance, and the uttermost part of the earth for Thy possession." He arrogates to himself the power of God. "Then saith Jesus unto him, Get thee hence, Satan : for it is written, Thou shalt worship the Lord thy God, and Him only shalt thou serve." And in these words Christ teaches us the impossibility of compromising with evil. No man can serve God and Mammon. " He that is not with Me," He said afterwards, " is against Me, and he that gathereth not with Me scattereth abroad."

III.

The Miracle of Cana.*

S. JOHN II. 1, 2.

" And the third day there was a marriage in Cana of Galilee ; and the mother of Jesus was there: and both Jesus was called, and His disciples, to the marriage."

AFTER the Temptation, our Lord re-joined His disciples, of whom there were then five, by Jordan, and with them started for Cana of Galilee. His newly-acquired disciple, Nathanael Bar-Tolmai, was of Cana (John xxi. 2), and it is possible that His journey thither may have had some connexion with Nathanael having joined himself to Him.

It is a three days' journey from Jordan, at Ænon, where John was baptizing, to Cana, which lies about four hours' walk north of Nazareth. The road taken by the Lord was through the Wadi Fuwar, by Ai and Bethel, to the main high road leading to Damascus. Christ had with Him, as already said, five disciples only—John and Andrew, Peter, Philip and Nathanael.† No doubt that Jesus went first to

* Suitable for the Second Sunday after the Epiphany.

† The Babylon Talmud also says that He had five disciples, but gives their names wrong, Sanh. 43, 1—Matthias, Nakai, Nezor, Bonai, and Thoda. Thoda is Thaddæus. Nakai is perhaps Nathanael.

Nazareth, thence His mother had been invited to Cana to the marriage, and He followed her thither. The way from Nazareth leads through low hills to the high marshy plain of Asochir, covered with bullrushes, abounding in tortoises and frogs, and with innumerable mosquitoes. About half an hour's walk from this swamp, lies the little village of Cana of Galilee, called at present, as of old, Kana el Gelil, that is—in Galilee. Behind the place rises the mountain, as a precipitous wall in a wide arc.*

The village can never have been of much consequence ; at the present day the houses in it are small and ruinous, and the place uninhabited. It lies at the watershed between the sea of Gennesareth and the Mediterranean, and this is the reason of the swampy nature of the soil.

Among the Jews no marriages were allowed to take place at the three great festivals, and Ezra had ordered that a marriage with a maiden should take place on a Wednesday, one with a widow on a Thursday. The marriage took place seven days after the betrothal, and for thirty days after the marriage the newly-wedded woman bore the title of Bride.

At the betrothal the bridegroom gave the bride a coin, and she presented him with a stone tablet, as a token that the marriage between man and woman was a figure of that union between God and the Jewish Church which was sealed

* The rival claim is made by Kefr Kenna, a castle-like village on a height.

on Sinai when the Tables of the Law were given. At a divorce these stone tablets were broken.

On the marriage morning the bridegroom sent the bridal dresses to his stepfather's house, together with ointments, fruits, and other presents. The bride, on her side, sent the bridegroom his winding sheet, which he was bound to put on twice in the year: on New Year's Day, and on the great Day of Atonement. When the bride was adorned by her friends, then the bridegroom came, crowned with flowers, and accompanied by his friends, to her house, whence he conducted her to his own, accompanied by flute players, song, and dances. Ten virgins carrying lamps formed the escort of the bride (Kallah); and ten young men carrying torches attended the bridegroom (Chathan); at the head of these latter was the groom's man, "the friend of the bridegroom," as he is termed in the Gospel. The attendants, and one as bride's man, chosen from the brothers of the bride, were called "Children of the Bridechamber," and their duties lasted through life, they were called in when quarrels ensued, to reconcile husband and wife together. At the wedding they saw to the wedding feast, and to the comfort and cheerfulness of the guests.

At the feast, a goblet of wine was provided, and the bridegroom and bride drank out of it, and then it was dashed to pieces on the ground, and the fragments were given to the guests.

The bride was closely veiled, richly adorned, and crowned with roses and myrtle; as Galilee was famous for the finely-woven linen made there, no doubt the bride on the occasion of the marriage at which Jesus was, was arrayed in linen, white, and clean, and fine. Salt was strewn as a crown on the head of bride and bridegroom. During the feast, songs were sung, and nuts were thrown to the children.

" And when they wanted wine, the mother of Jesus saith unto Him, They have no wine. Jesus saith unto her, Woman, what have I to do with thee? Mine hour is not yet come. His mother saith unto the servants, Whatsoever He saith unto you, Do it. And there were set there six waterpots of stone, after the manner of the purifying of the Jews, containing two or three firkins apiece. Jesus saith unto them, Fill the waterpots with water. And they filled them up to the brim. And He saith unto them, Draw out now, and bear unto the governor of the feast. And they bare it."

The strict Jews washed their hands not only before midday meal and supper (Luke xi. 38), but also whenever they ate bread (Matt. xv. 2), and were very scrupulous about the washing of every vessel used for food. (Mark vii. 2 ; Matt. xxiii. 25.) As knives and forks were dispensed with in eating, and everyone helped himself from the dish with his fingers, it was absolutely necessary that the hand should be scrupulously clean.

The marriage at Cana was a marriage of people in poor

circumstances. The Galilæans were mostly a poor people, they drank very little wine and milk. Probably the guests brought their small contributions to the feast, and the ruler of the feast, or groom's man, had reckoned on some of them giving wine, but—all at once it was found that the poor little store of the fruit of the grape was out. Mary, with the tender, kindly, woman's heart, felt for the poor young people, and the humiliation on this, the greatest day of their life, of being unable to provide sufficient wine for all who were invited. Then she comes to her Divine Son, and whispers, "They have no wine." Perhaps she thought of what Elijah had done for his hostess, the widow of Sarepta, whose oil and meal he had multiplied, or of the blessing given by Elisha to the oil vessel of the Shunammite.

But the Lord refused to have His hand forced. Satan had endeavoured, a few days previously, to force Him to manifest His Divine power, and now His mother appears to urge Him to do the same. Yet how different are the cases ! Satan would have Him change stones into bread to satisfy His own bodily requirements ; stones, into a necessary of life. Here He is asked to provide what is no necessary, but a luxury.

His answer to His mother is, " Woman, what have I to do with thee ? Mine hour is not yet come." There is no reproach in the title, Woman. With it He addressed her from the Cross, " Woman, behold thy son." But the other words imply that His period of subjection to His mother was at an end. Hitherto He had yielded to her will, and followed her advice, now He has no more to do with her. He has His mission to fulfil, the Will of His Heavenly Father to do, and that alone must be His governing principle.

But Mary's faith is not shaken. She goes to the servants, and bids them do whatsoever He commands. Then He ordered the waterpots to be filled with water, and the fluid poured forth and taken to the groom's man. " When the ruler of the feast had tasted the water that was made wine, and knew not whence it was : (but the servants which drew the water knew ;) the governor of the feast called the bridegroom, and saith unto him, Every man at the beginning doth set forth good wine ; and when men have well drunk, then that which is worse : but thou hast kept the good wine until now."

The best Palestinian wine is dark red, and sweet ; it is held far superior to the white, which is often coloured to make it pass as the red wine. This red wine is, however, so strong, that, as a rule, it is not drunk without admixture with water.*

S. John does not give an account of the Temptation. The other evangelists do not give an account of the miracle

---

* Sabbat. f. 79—" Raba said, That is no wine, which is not mixed with three parts of water." As a rule, however, two-thirds were of water. Sanhed. f. 14.

of Cana ; and yet how one follows on the other and completes the picture.

Christ refuses to change a stone into bread to satisfy Himself ; He transforms water into wine to relieve the anxiety of, and to gratify others. He refused to be urged to work a miracle by Satan. He refuses to be forced to work a miracle by His mother.

In Psalm cxxviii. a wife is likened to a fruitful vine, on the walls of a house. In the Eastern Church, at the betrothal, the priest, holding a glass of wine in his hand, recites this psalm.

The marriage of Cana, in which water is converted into wine, at the outset of Christ's ministry, is a figure of His betrothal to His Church at the Last Supper, at the close of His ministry, when He changed wine into His Blood.

By this miracle Christ emphatically declared that use was to be made of all the good things God had created, and that no fanatical narrowness must protest against any. He consecrated the use of wine, and He consecrated marriage ; and, as some fanatics have declared against marriage as sinful, so have others declared against wine. Christ shewed by His presence at Cana, and His first miracle, that no institution, and no gift of God is to be absolutely rejected because it is capable of abuse. In wine there lurks a danger, and in all fermented liquor. Noah drank, and was drunken, and heathenism deified wine, and made of drunkenness divine excitation. The heathen world sanctioned polygamy, and fell into abominable licence. Christ preaches in this, His first miracle, the lesson of moderation; let every man have his one wife, and be faithful to her; and let the good things of this world be used, and not be abused.

I have said that this miracle follows on the Temptation, and completes its lessons. It does so in another way to those already mentioned.

Satan shewed Christ, in a vision, the glory of the world, and promised to give it Him at present, but said nothing about the future; contrasting himself with God, Who, from the same mount, shewed Moses the promised land, and gave it him not, but laid on him only the burden of bringing the people of Israel through the wilderness to its confines.

And now the master of the feast follows on the same thought unconsciously. " Every man at the beginning doth set forth good wine, and—then that which is worse, but thou hast kept the good wine until now." In these words he shews, without knowing it, the difference between man's and Satan's dealings, and God's dealings. Satan gives present delight and gladness, but after misery. God gives sorrow and trial now, but after that an exceeding weight of glory. Tears come first, then laughter : struggle first, then victory. As Bishop Jeremy Taylor said, " First penitents, and then communicants ; first waters of sorrow, and then the wine of the chalice ; first the justifications of correction, and then the sanctifications of the Sacrament, and the effects of Divine power, joy, and peace, and serenity, hopes full of confidence, and confidence without shame, and boldness without presumption : for Jesus keeps the best wine till the last, not only because of the direct reservation of the highest joys till the nearer approaches of glory, but also, because our relishes are higher after a long fruition than at the first essays ; such being the nature of grace, that it increases in relish as it does in fruition, every part of grace being new duty and new reward."

IV

The Proclamation.

S. LUKE IV. 21.

" This day is this Scripture fulfilled in your ears."

AFTER the Miracle of Cana, our Lord probably returned to Nazareth, but He visited Capernaum, and the shores of the Lake of Gennesareth occasionally, for there Andrew, Peter, and John lived, and pursued their avocation as fishers. He visited them, but did not call them from their business till John was cast into prison by Herod. "From that time," says S. Matthew, "Jesus began to preach, and to say, Repent : for the kingdom of Heaven is at hand" (iv. 17). S. Luke says that after the temptation, "Jesus returned in the power of the Spirit into Galilee : and there went out a fame of Him through all the region round about. And He taught in their synagogues, being glorified of all." Then S. Luke goes on to say that He came to Nazareth, and there, in the synagogue, proclaimed His mission, which so incensed the people of Nazareth that they sought to take His life. S. John, directly after the account of the Miracle of Cana, says, "After this He went down to Capernaum, He, and His mother, and His brethren, and His disciples : and they continued there not many days " (ii. 12). We cannot be wrong in judging that this removal of the whole family ensued on the proclamation of the Gospel in the synagogue at Nazareth, and the consequent attempt on His life. Capernaum became the home of His manhood, as Nazareth had been the home of His youth. He was forced to leave Nazareth, but He did not leave it till driven from it by the envy and wounded pride of the men there. "He came unto His own, and His own received Him not."

Probably the arrest of S. John the Baptist took place shortly after Christ had been baptized. Then, at once, Christ began His ministry, and He began it by announcing Who He was, and what He had come to do, in the synagogue of His own city Nazareth. That, however, He had performed some marvellous works at Capernaum already, perhaps when on a visit to His disciples, Andrew and Peter, we learn from the words of the Jews at Nazareth. What these works were we do not know. The Gospels are silent concerning them.

Let us now consider the formal, solemn announcement with which He opened His missionary labours of three years. This is given by S. Luke very fully.

" He came to Nazareth, where He had been brought up : and, as His custom was, He went into the synagogue on the Sabbath day, and stood up to read. And there was delivered unto Him the book of the prophet Esaias. And when He had opened the book, He found the place where it was written, The Spirit of the Lord is upon Me, because He hath anointed Me to preach the Gospel to the poor ; He hath sent Me to heal the broken-hearted, to preach deliverance to the captives, and recovering of sight to the blind, to set at liberty them that are bruised, to preach the acceptable year of the Lord. And He closed the book, and He gave it again to the minister, and sat down. And the eyes of all them that were in the synagogue were fastened on Him. And He began to say unto them, This day is this Scripture fulfilled in your ears. And all bare Him witness, and wondered at the gracious words which proceeded out of His mouth."

As our Blessed Lord came to the Jew first, and only when the Jew rejected Him was the Gospel carried to the Gentile, so, apparently, was it now. He had indeed preached " Repent ye, for the kingdom of Heaven is at hand," in the synagogues round, and in that of His own city, but now He made His first declaration of His mission in His own city to His own citizens, and only when they rejected Him, did He remove elsewhere and announce the glad tidings to others. If this be as I suppose, it is surely a lesson to us always to begin to do good to those who are near and around us, to make the sphere in which we find ourselves the sphere of our proper work. We must begin at the centre of our little circle and work outwards.

A synagogue generally stood on the highest piece of ground in a city, or near it; it was oblong, and the end opposite to the entrance pointed towards Jerusalem. There were the seats of the elders, and in the midst, at this end, was the ark with a lamp always burning before it, in which was preserved the roll of the Law. Before it also was an eight-branched candlestick, lighted on the highest festivals. A little way down was a raised platform, on which several persons could stand at once, and in the middle rose a pulpit, in which the reader stood to read those lessons which were not from the books of Moses. The roll of the Law was taken with great solemnity out of the ark, and unrolled by the Rabbi, so that the congregation might not look on the writing. The lessons from Moses were so arranged that the books of the Law were read through once in three years. Much less ceremony was shown about the second lesson, which was taken from the prophets and historical books. On week days, not less than twenty-one verses were read, on the Sabbath, not more than three, five, or seven.* After this lesson followed the exposition, or interpretation.

The Scriptures were read in Hebrew, but the Hebrew was unintelligible to the Jews after their return from the Babylonish captivity, consequently the interpreter translated or expounded what he had read in the Aramaic or Syro-Chaldee tongue.

* Massechat Sopherim, c. 12.

The reader stood when reading the prophets, but was allowed to sit or stand for the historical books.

Our Lord read in Hebrew, and explained in Aramaic, but He also spoke Greek, and S. Mark has preserved in his Gospel several of our Lord's sayings, which were clearly spoken in the Greek tongue, some in the vernacular.* The ten cities, Decapolis, in Galilee were Greek towns, and throughout Galilee there was so large an admixture of Greeks that it was necessary—or almost necessary—to know both, much as in Wales, English and Welsh are spoken, or in Belgium, Flemish and French.

Originally the prophets and historical books had not been read in the synagogue service, but when Antiochus Epiphanes forbade the reading of the Law, in the services of the Sabbath, the prophets and other books had been substituted for those of Moses, and when this restriction was withdrawn the Jews continued reading the prophets, but read the Law as well, as of old, in the place of honour. The prophets and historical books were not kept in the ark, but in a cupboard beside the pulpit.

The minister, or servant of the synagogue, took the Book out of the cupboard, and handed it to the reader, and stood by him to nudge him, or whisper to him when to stop, or

* iii. 18 ; v. 41 ; vii. 11, 34 ; xiv. 36 ; xv. 34 ; also S. Matt. xvi. 18 ; xxvii. 46; Christ also spoke with Pilate, who almost certainly did not use Aramaic, but Greek.

to correct him if he mispronounced a word. Our Blessed Lord then, in the synagogue, ascended the pulpit, and the minister handed Him the roll. He opened the roll at Isaiah, and read the lesson appointed for the Day of Atonement.

As long as our Lord preached about generalities, the hearers approved and wondered at the gracious words that proceeded out of His mouth; but He speedily came to particulars, then they said, "Is not this Joseph's son? And He said unto them, Ye will surely say unto Me this proverb, Physician, heal Thyself: whatsoever we have heard done in Capernaum, do also here in Thy country. And He said, Verily I say unto you, No prophet is accepted in his own country. But I tell you of a truth, many widows were in Israel in the days of Elias, when the heaven was shut up three years and six months, when great famine was throughout all the land; but unto none of them was Elias sent, save unto Sarepta, a city of Sidon, unto a woman that was a widow. And many lepers were in Israel in the time of Eliseus the prophet; and none of them was cleansed, saving Naaman the Syrian. And all they in the synagogue, when they heard these things, were filled with wrath, and rose up, and thrust Him out of the city, and led Him unto the brow of the hill whereon their city was built, that they might cast Him down headlong. But He passing through the midst of them went His way." (S. Luke iv. 14-30.)

c

When our Lord began to make personal application of the passage, then the dissatisfaction of the audience broke forth, and they tumultuously broke up the service, and carried Him to the precipice to fling Him down. In Bethlehem He had been denied a place in the inn, here in Nazareth He is rejected.

Of old, under king Amaziah, had the Jews put a large number of Edomites to death in the same way.

" Ten thousand left alive did the children of Judah carry away captive, and brought them unto the top of the rock, and cast them down from the top of the rock, that they all were broken in pieces." (2 Chron. xxv. 12.)

Nazareth is called in the Talmud the " white city on a mountain," because it lies on a height, and is built of the white limestone of the rock. Nazareth is on one of the spurs of Lebanon, just where they fall away into the plain of Esdraelon. The prevalent opinion at the present day at Nazareth is that Christ was dragged out of the town to a rocky height about two miles off, but this is not consonant with the words of S. Luke, who says that the precipice was that of the rock on which the town was built, and, indeed, there is a very remarkable precipice, almost perpendicular, and forty or fifty feet high, close outside the walls, not far from the present mean synagogue, which probably stands on the site of the old one in which Christ taught; and it is almost certain that this was the identical cliff

over which His infuriated townsmen attempted to hurl
Him.

But the power was not given to these wretched men,
blinded with pride and passion, to hurt the Lord's anointed.
How He escaped them we do not know; perhaps they
were blinded like the Syrians, who compassed the little
city in which was Elisha; or perhaps He vanished out
of their sight.

What was actually the cause of the sudden upboil of these
men's wrath? It was that their self-esteem was wounded.
Christ declared that only the humble and meek would be
able to receive Him. Elijah was persecuted, and received
only by one poor widow. Naaman was unworthy to be healed
till he humbled himself to dip in despised Jordan. The
men of Nazareth understood the inferences. It was not
flattering to their pride; they could not be fed and healed
unless they became humble, and submitted to the Lord's
Christ. This they would not do—and they cast Him out
of their city.

As with Christ, so with His Church, and with His mes-
sengers. As long as they preach a Gospel which does not
touch man's pride and lower his self-esteem they wonder at
the graciousness of the Gospel, but the moment it bids them
not to be wise in their own conceits, insists on submission
of the entire man, body, soul, and reason to Christ, and
calls to a lowly walk and self-abasement, then men rise up

against the Church, and its minister, and—against the true
Gospel of Christ, and would, if they could, cast it out of
their city, and hurl it from their thoughts.*

* The only difficulty in arranging the sequence of events springs from
the passage of S. Mark vi. 1-4, where Jesus is said to have taught in the
synagogue, "in His own country," and to have quoted the same proverb,
"A prophet is not without honour but in his own country, and among his
own kin, and in his own house," and this S. Mark gives *after* the calling of
the Apostles on the lake, the cure of the demoniac, of S. Peter's wife's
mother, and the raising of Jairus' daughter. But S. Mark does not specify
Nazareth by name; and after leaving Nazareth, Capernaum became His
"own city," and there is no reason why the same proverb should not be
quoted more than once. It was as applicable at Capernaum and elsewhere,
where He was known, as at Nazareth.

V.

Gennesareth.

S. MARK II. 1.

"He entered into Capernaum."

AFTER the men of Nazareth had made an attempt on the life of Christ, it was no longer safe for Him to remain in the little town. He therefore moved with His mother and brethren to Capernaum, on the Lake of Gennesareth. S. John says, "He went down" (κατέβη), and the expression is just. The Jews divided Galilee into three parts—Higher Galilee, which was above the height to which the sycamore grew, Lower Galilee, where the wild fig trees grew, and the Deep Land. Nazareth lies in Lower Galilee, about two hours' journey from the capital, Tiberias, which Herod Antipas called after the Emperor Tiberius. Nazareth stands some 1,350 feet above the lake, and the descent from the elevated table-land is by a steep road of half an hour's rapid fall, to a point where the road divides, one way leading to Capernaum, the other to Tiberias. The view from the high table-land, before the road goes down, is wonderfully beautiful. A sparkling sheet of water enclosed by hills, with precipitous edges, and above, to the north, the snowy

peak of Hermon, and away to the east the bold, barren
ranges of the mountains of Hauran. The Sea of Galilee,
or Lake of Gennesareth, lies 700 feet below the level
of the ocean, and this depression makes the basin in
which the lake lies very hot, in summer excessively so,
but in spring the air there is balmy and mild. Of old, it
was the most populous part of Palestine. No less than
nine cities stood on the shores of the lake, which were then
by no means so barren as now. Most of our Lord's public
life was spent in the environs of the Sea of Gennesareth,
and we may therefore consider a little more closely its
aspect and character.

The original population of the shores of. the lake was
Sidonian, and when Tyre and Sidon were founded on the
shores of the Mediterranean they moved westward, but the
town of Bethsidon still retained the name given it by its
first inhabitants. The richest part of the shores was at the
north-west, where is a luxuriant plain of half-moon shape,
walled out from the north and west winds by mountains,
and exposed to the sun. This was where the princes and
the nobles had their country residences, and the gardens
were filled with all kinds of flowers and fruit. The lake was
called by its first colonists, Cennereth, or the Harp, from its
shape. The Jews thought so highly of its beauty that they
said, " God created seven seas—but for Himself He elected
but one, and that the lake Gennesareth ;" and again, " It is

the Gate of Paradise." Josephus says, " It is a district where Nature seems to have constrained herself to create an eternal spring, and to gather into one spot the products of every zone." To the present day the date-palm, citrons, pomegranate, indigo, rice, sugar-cane, grow there, cotton, balsams, vines, thrive, the purple grapes are as big as plums, and the bunches weigh twelve pounds. Here also the fig tree yields her fruit throughout the year, ripening every month. The Jews call Gennesareth the Garden Lake, and if there were any place in Palestine that could recall the lost Paradise, it was this fruitful, beautiful tract, watered with its five streams.

At Chammath, about two miles south of Tiberias, are hot springs, of old much used for baths, and half an hour's walk above Tiberias a cold spring of beautiful water bursts out of the mountain side, and pours down to the lake in five or six streams. At Tabigha also are hot springs, that gush steaming down into the blue waters of the lake.

Now the neglect and mismanagement of the Turkish Government have led to the devastation of this beautiful corner of the world, and many of the foreign plants once introduced into it have died out, or are disappearing. We can only guess what a garden of delight it must have been in the time of our Lord, when the aqueducts were in working order, and canals carried water to all the gardens and fields.

Capernaum—at present called Tell-Hum, was the place

where the prophet Nahum was buried. The name signifies the Village of Nahum. It is now a heap of ruins of buildings erected out of basalt, black and dismal ; a contrast to the bright limestone of Nazareth.

A good number of springs rise about it. Among the ruins are the white marble remains of some handsome building, probably a synagogue—that built by the Roman centurion of whom mention is made by S. Luke (vii. 5). Near it are the remains of what is believed to be an old Christian church. There are no traces of the port.

Here, at Capernaum, Jesus was safe. A little boat carried Him when He willed over the sea into the tetrarchy of Ituræa ; if He ascended the heights to the north-west, and crossed the mountain shoulder, He was in the region of Tyre and Sidon. Capernaum lay, then, conveniently situated for the mission Christ had to fulfil, a place whence He could easily travel into three districts. What, however, also, no doubt, conduced to Christ making His home there was that it was the residence of Simon Peter, who was the oldest of His disciples. Capernaum is not mentioned in the Old Testament. It was of sufficient size to be always called a " city "; had its own synagogue, which was built by the centurion of the detachment of Roman soldiers quartered in the place. Besides the garrison, it had also a customs' station, where the dues were gathered both by stationary and by itinerant officers.

Capernaum is called especially Christ's "own city," and
S. Mark says that when He returned thither from His
journeys, He was "at home." (ii. 1.)* It lay on the great
trade road from Damascus, and through it passed the wares
of Syria and Phœnicia ; and this "way of the sea" is that mentioned by Isaiah (ix. 1). The main road here came down
from the high land and led south to Samaria and Jerusalem.

"And Jesus, walking by the sea of Galilee, saw two
brethren, Simon, called Peter, and Andrew, his brother,
casting a net into the sea : for they were fishers. And He
said unto them, Follow Me, and I will make you fishers of
men. And they straightway left their nets and followed
Him. And going on from thence, He saw other two
brethren, James, the son of Zebedee, and John, his brother,
in a ship with Zebedee, their father, mending their nets ;
and He called them. And they immediately left their ship
and their father, and followed Him." (S. Matt. iv. 18-22 ;
S. Mark i. 16-20.)

Our Lord had just come from Nazareth, and He walked
round the shores of the sea (περιπατῶν), which to the west
form a bay between Tiberias and Capernaum.† The road
from Nazareth comes steeply down the hill at Magdala, the

* Nazareth was His Mecca, Capernaum His Medina.

† From the south end of the lake to the hot springs is one hour ; thence
to Tiberias, 35 minutes ; thence to Magdala, 1 hour and 10 minutes; to
Khan Minyeh (Tarichea) one hour ; Tell-Hum, 1 hour and 5 minutes ;
Jordan, 1 hour and 5 minutes.

birth-place of Mary Magdalen, and thence our Lord had a
walk of three hours and a quarter to Capernaum, along the
shore of the sea. He passed the little town of Tarichea.
Beyond this at the present day are some ruins, which some
travellers have supposed to be the remains of Bethsaida,
the birth-place of S. Peter, and here a narrow road or path
now runs, close to the water's edge, after having crossed a
height above the lake. Here it was, probably, that Christ
came on the boat of Peter and Andrew. We know from
S. John's Gospel that they had already been brought to
know Christ, for He had been pointed out to them by the
Baptist, and they had returned with Him from Jordan till
their roads divided at Bethshean, and He had gone west to
Nazareth, and they north to the lake. Now He calls them,
and they manifest no surprise. It was the same with the
the sons of Zebedee ; the only one of these who had not
been called, and did not know Christ, was S. James.

Since the conquest of Canaan by Joshua, all Israelites
were allowed to fish with the hook in the Sea of Galilee,
but the children of Naphtali only were allowed to use nets.*
The portion of Naphtali extended from the Jordan down
the west side of the sea to a little above the site of the
city Tiberias, built long after. Our Lord had the sons of
Alphæus also with Him, these were James the Less, Judas
also called Lebbæus, Simon the Canaanite, and Joseph or

* Bava Kama, f. 81.

Joses. These were all sons of Cleopas, who is believed to have been the brother of Joseph, Christ's foster-father,* and are called His brethren. Their mother's name was Mary.

S. Mark also says that Levi, or Matthew, was a son of Alphæus, but hardly of the same. Alphæus is the Greek pronunciation of the name Chelphai, or Chelpha. The Galilæans pronounced the guttural letter Cheth roughly, and this letter was usually omitted by the Greeks when turning a Hebrew name into Greek.† Joses, the youngest of these brothers, was probably not of age at the time, afterwards he was proposed with Matthias to become an Apostle after the fall of Judas. Both he and James bore the honourable designation of " the Just." The name of Barsabas is given to him and to Judas Thaddæus, that is, " the son of the old man," that old man being Cleopas or Alphæus.

And now if we would draw a lesson from the call of the Apostles, it is not hard to find it. We are struck with the promptness with which they forsook all and followed Christ. They threw aside their nets, they left their ships, and obeyed His call instantly. Whenever we know that a duty has to be performed, let us not put off the doing of it to a more convenient season, but do it at once. A duty postponed is half neglected.

* Hegesippus, quoted by Eusebius, says so, and Hegesippus was a writer of the second century.

† For instance, Chagai becomes in Greek 'Αγγαῖος, Chazael becomes 'Αζαήλ, Chabor is 'Αβώρ.

VI

The Sabbath at Capernaum.

S. MARK I. 21.

" Straightway on the Sabbath day He entered into the synagogue, and taught."

THE week after the expulsion from Nazareth was probably spent by our Lord at Capernaum, in finding a house, and settling His mother into it, together with His cousins, the sons of Alphæus, who shared His banishment.

But when the Sabbath came, He went, as was His wont, to the synagogue. This was, probably, the white marble, newly-erected synagogue, built by the Roman centurion, the ruins of which, with Corinthian pillars broken and strewn about, remain to this day above the dingy black fragments of walls of the old town.

I have already described the service of the synagogue, but I will here say a few words about the organization of the Jewish community for worship, because we see in that the rudiments of the structure of the Christian Church.

Wherever there were 120 Jews, there a synagogue was erected, and the existence of a synagogue raised a place from being a village to be a city.* In the synagogue, at

* Sanhed. f. 17, 2.

the Jerusalem end, sat the elders, in number ten, who formed the council; with these were three men who managed the secular affairs of the community, looked after the funds belonging to the synagogue, its repairs, and so forth.

Beside these was the Chazan, Bishop or Angel, who offered the public prayers, watched over the correct reading of the Law, and called on some of the congregation to read the minor lessons, and precented the hymns. Beside the Chazan, were three Parnasin, or Deacons, two of whom were employed in collecting the alms for the poor, and the third in distributing them. Only a Priest, or Cohen, might give the blessing, and he did so by first blessing those on his right, with raised right hand, then those on his left, and lastly those before him. Any Rabbi present, or stranger, might be called on by the Chazan, or ruler of the synagogue, to explain the lesson and preach.

We see in this constitution of the synagogue the elements of Church order. The elders of the synagogue were afterwards represented by the presbyters, the Chazan by the bishop, and the Parnasin by the deacons.

The Sabbath had come; a day of rest after the week of changing homes, the trouble and discomfort of settling into a new house. Thrice, from the roof of the synagogue, a trumpet blast announced the Sabbath at sunset—the first blast to warn those in the fields to desist from labour, the second to call those in the city to give up their work, the third to call all householders to kindle the sabbatical lamp. Christ went at once to the synagogue, where the community had assembled. There the perpetual light was burning before the ark that contained the law.

The service began with hymn and prayer; there were eighteen prayers or collects, and then began the lessons. The ruler of the synagogue called on Jesus to expound, "And they were astonished at His doctrine, for His word was with power." (S. Luke iv. 32.) " He taught them as one that had authority, and not as the scribes." (S. Mark i. 22.) We have in the Talmud a vast collection of the teaching of the Rabbis of that, of earlier, and of later time, and we know pretty well what was its character. It consisted of a mass of trivialities, word-torturings, wringing out of Scripture commands never given, and finding in it reasons for Rabbinical traditions and precepts, which are no reasons at all to sane men.

What a contrast was Christ's downright, plain, pure doctrine to this! It was like the waft of a cool breeze from the snows of Hermon into the hot steamy swelter by the lake in midsummer.

Suddenly—in the midst of His discourse, whilst there was silence, and all hung on His lips, there came an interruption of an unusual nature, different from that which had disturbed His discourse on the previous Sabbath. "There was in their synagogue a man with an unclean spirit; and he cried

out, saying, Let us alone ; what have we to do with Thee,
Thou Jesus of Nazareth ? art Thou come to destroy us ?
I know Thee, Who Thou art ; the Holy One of God."
(S. Mark i. 23, 24 ; S. Luke iv. 33, 34.)

The Holy Spirit at Jordan had borne testimony to Christ ;
the inanimate element, water, had given witness to Him at
Cana ; and now the evil spirit is constrained to declare Him.

There is something very significant in the outcry of the
possessed man.   This was the first miracle Christ wrought
after He had announced His mission, and now the devil
confesses that this mission of the Son of God is the expulsion of the Evil One, the destruction of the power of the
devil.   The demoniac was typical of the whole of humanity
possessed with the Spirit of Evil since the Fall, a spirit
driving mankind into horrible uncleanness, and atrocious
cruelties.   Christ was come to destroy the works of the
devil, to free mankind from his power, to expel the evil from
the world, and recover human nature from its bondage
and subjection.   The evil spirit knows this, and proclaims
it aloud in the synagogue of Capernaum.   Christ had
announced His mission the previous Sabbath at Nazareth,
and He had been expelled the city and synagogue.   Now
the devil proclaims it, and Christ casts forth the devil.

Consider for a moment the scene.   It was the Sabbath
eve service ; the sun had set, dusk had settled in on the
building, but the red light shone by the ark, and by it the

faces of the congregation were dimly seen turned to the preacher; then, all at once, in the gathering darkness, from a corner, come shrill cries and shrieks, and a madman bounds into the middle of the congregation, foaming at the mouth, brandishing his arms, then pointing to Christ, Who stands on the platform, and declares that He is the Holy One of God, sent to drive away evil spirits, and destroy their power over men.

When the man with the unclean spirit cried out, "I know Thee, Who Thou art, the Holy One of God," he used a general paraphrastic expression for Jehovah. So in Daniel (ix. 24), Messiah is called "the Holy of Holies."

Was this outcry by constraint, unwilling, or was it treacherous? That we can hardly decide. Our Lord silenced the possessed; He did not need the testimony of devils; S. Mark says, "He suffered not the devils to speak, because they knew Him" (i. 34). It may have been that these foul spirits by proclaiming Him sought to bring Him into disrepute, by apparently making common cause with Him, acting as His witnesses, and so giving occasion to the Pharisees to say as they actually did, "He casteth out devils through Beelzebub, the prince of devils." (S. Matt. xii. 24.) But it is more probable that the testimony was unwillingly wrung from them, that impotent rage and hate carried them away, and forced them to shriek forth the truth, and with it to break into horrible blasphemies.

The question must always present itself to us, when we read of possession in the New Testament, what it was in our Lord's time, and whether it still exists. Nowadays we are inclined to look to physical and material causes for all maladies, and to regard a suggestion that demoniacal agency may be at work among men as a question of superstition. Yet, perhaps, we are exaggerating the influence of physical derangement on mental aberration. Man is given reason as his guide, to hold the reins of passion and guide his course. If he allows reason in little matters to be unseated, and gives way to caprice, then something else will assume the direction. We speak of a man being full of the spirit of pride, or self-conceit, or the spirit of uncleanness, or intemperance. May it not be that where he wilfully allows his vanity, or his passions, to run away with him, that an evil spirit may take possession of him so completely that reason no longer is able to recover control?

This man with the unclean spirit was not so bad but that he was allowed to be one of the regular congregation on the Sabbath. His friends knew him only as a foulminded fellow, whose talk was obscene, whose jokes were not fit to listen to, who had a twist of the brain, which caused him to find some disgusting suggestion in whatever he heard, or saw, or read. It was no worse than that. The Jews at Nazareth were also possessed but with another spirit—the spirit of pride ; having long yielded to self-com-

D

placency, they had lost the faculty of seeing their own short-comings, they were self-opinionated, self-righteous ; whatsoever things they did were right, whatsoever things they said were wise, they could not suppose themselves to be in the wrong, they were absolutely blind to their own ignorance and unworthiness.

Are there not many nowadays possessed with this same spirit ? I think we meet them continually, people with an inordinate opinion of themselves. So there are men nowadays who have fallen under the possession of other spirits —the spirit of uncleanness, the lying spirit, the spirit of intemperance, the spirit of envy, the discontented, murmuring spirit.

Where these are yielded to, they become masters, and take full possession.

Our Lord expelled the spirits from the possessed, and He did so to show that with Him is the power to control all evil spirits, and that if any man feels an infirmity making him prone to yield to this or that spirit, he must seek of Christ the strength to enable his reason to sit firm, and check his natural proclivities, and so discipline his will, and mould his habits, that evil may not gain dominion over him.

At the baptism of every Christian the question is asked, " Dost thou renounce the devil and all his works, the vain pomp and glory of the world, with all covetous desires of the same, and the carnal desires of the flesh, so that thou wilt not follow, nor be led by them?" That is to say, the duty is imposed on every son of God to exercise the most thorough, just, and rational control over his actions. He must not drift along, a prey to his animal passions, or be drawn along by the seductions of the world. If he remains governed by the reason, enlightened by the Divine Spirit, he is living as a Christian; but if he allows the world or the flesh to control him, then the Evil Spirit obtains power over him, and gradually enchains and displaces reason, or reason is only employed as the servant of evil.

After the possessed in the synagogue had confessed Christ, "Jesus rebuked him, saying, Hold thy peace, and come out of him." Then the devil left the man. "When the devil had thrown him in the midst, he came out of him and hurt him not. And they were all amazed, and spake among themselves, saying, What a word is this! for with authority and power He commandeth the unclean spirits, and they come out."

After the sermon in the Sabbath service, the Chazan begins again, and says the Holy, Holy, Holy, and gives thanks to God, to which the people respond with "Thanks be to Thee, O God," and with Amen. Then the priest turns to the people and gives the blessing.

Apparently, on this occasion, the congregation broke up in excitement when the demoniac was healed, without waiting for the conclusion.

" And immediately His fame spread abroad throughout all the region round about Galilee. And forthwith, when they were come out of the synagogue, they entered into the house of Simon and Andrew, with James and John, but Simon's wife's mother lay sick of a fever ; and anon they tell Him of her. And He came, and took her by the hand, and lifted her up ; and immediately the fever left her, and she ministered unto them."

Near the water's edge, among the ruins of Capernaum, are the remains of what was, apparently, an ancient Christian Church, and we know that many centuries ago, before the place fell to decay, the house of Peter was converted into a Church. These poor remains, overgrown with grass and thorns, may be the traces of the church, standing on the site of the fisherman's cottage, where the miracle of healing Peter's wife's mother was performed.

Peter was a native of Bethsaida ; his father, Jonas, was dead, and probably he had moved into his wife's little property at Capernaum, where her mother lived with them.

Whether the possessed was healed in the beginning of the Sabbath, that is, after sunset on Friday, or on Saturday morning, we do not know, but perhaps it was at the first Sabbath service on the eve, then S. Peter's wife's mother was restored directly after, and the rumour of the miracles spread all through the neighbourhood that still Sabbath day.

" The fever left her." Christ shows Himself as the

cooling, soothing power, Who can subdue all wild pulsations of the heart. He drove out the unclean spirit, and He brings the heated, fevered body to calmness. All passion is a fever ; and continued yielding to passion results in possession. Christ shows that He is to be had recourse to in the beginning of ills, as well as when evil has taken full hold. Whenever there is light temptation, when the pulse throbs, and the cheek flushes, and the eye sparkles with passion, it is a sort of fever; then put the hand into the hand of Christ, and the passion subsides. So shall not Satan gain any dominion over you, so shall you be sure of never falling under the possession of the Spirit of Evil.

VII

The First Missionary Tour.

S. MATTHEW IV. 23.

" And Jesus went about all Galilee, teaching in their synagogues, and preaching the Gospel of the Kingdom."

OUR Blessed Lord had cast the devil out of the possessed man on the first Sabbath of His arrival and settlement at Capernaum after His expulsion from Nazareth. During the rest of that day, the fame of what He had done spread from mouth to mouth, so that the whole town and neighbourhood was full of excitement and impatience, till the sun set, and the trumpet blast from the synagogue roof announced that the Day of Rest was over. Then, immediately, the streets were thronged with people, all running in one direction. "At even," says S. Mark, "when the sun did set, they brought unto Him all that were diseased, and them that were possessed with devils. And all the city was gathered together at the door. And He healed many that were sick of divers diseases, and cast out many devils ; and suffered not the devils to speak, because they knew Him " (i. 32-34). S. Luke says much the same, " Now when the sun was setting, all they that had sick

with divers diseases brought them unto Him; and He laid
His hands on everyone of them. And devils also came
out of many, crying out and saying, Thou art Christ, the
Son of God. And He, rebuking them, suffered them not
to speak; for they knew that He was Christ" (iv. 40-1).

On the Sabbath the Jews were not suffered to carry their
sick, or, indeed, any burden, and not to go a journey of
more than two thousand paces. Consequently the people
of Capernaum waited for sundown before claiming the
aid of Christ for their sick friends and relatives.

So the night closed in. "And in the morning, rising up
a great while before day, He went out, and departed into
a solitary place, and there prayed. And Simon, and they
that were with him"—that is, Andrew, James, and John—
"followed after Him. And when they had found Him,
they said unto Him, All men seek for Thee. And He
said unto them, Let us go into the next town that I
may preach there also : for therefore came I forth." (S.
Mark i. 35-38.)

Behind Capernaum opens a glen, with the bed of a dry
rivulet in it, and above are the mountains. About an hour's
ride up the glen are the ruins of Chorazin.* Our Lord
probably, as was His wont, ascended the hill behind Capernaum, whence a beautiful view is to be had of the blue

* This agrees exactly with the distance given by Josephus : the modern
name preserves the old one, Keráze.

lake, and the Syrian mountains beyond.   There He prayed, and saw the white dawn steal up the sky from behind the broken outline on the east.

Chorazin was, no doubt, the first town visited by Christ when He started on His first missionary journey.   The ruins are partly in the valley, about a spring, and on a shoulder of the hill above, and are extensive.   The houses are fairly well preserved, are quadrangular, with the roofs supported on pillars.   The walls are all of black basalt. About an hour further up the valley, where the steep road reaches the level of the plateau, is the place where, according to ancient tradition, is the well into which Joseph was cast by his brethren.   The nearest town of any importance at present is Safed, a city lying high on a hill-top, originally fortified ; and regarded as one of the holy cities of the Jews. The Rabbis were wont to say that from only four cities, Jerusalem, Hebron, Safed, and Tiberias, did prayers ascend direct to the throne of God.   Safed is about three hours' journey from Capernaum, and as our Lord ascended towards it, the high-perched, fortified town on the mountain was before His eyes.   To it, almost certainly, He referred when He said, " A city set on a hill cannot be hid." (S. Matt. v. 14.)   It is the highest situated of all the cities of Palestine.

From Safed, Christ probably went to Meron, an important place, the residence of some famous Rabbis, contemporaries of our Lord.   Meron is an hour and a half west-north-west

of Safed. Thence He would, in all likelihood, have gone
to Kadesh Naphtali, abounding in hot springs ; where were
shown the tombs of Barak and Deborah. Thus would be
fulfilled the saying of the prophet Isaiah, to which the evan-
gelist refers as foretelling the events of this period. " The
land of Zabulon, and the land of Nephthalim, by the way of
the sea, beyond Jordan, Galilee of the Gentiles ; the people
which sat in darkness saw great light : and to them which
sat in the region and shadow of death, light is sprung up."
(S. Matt. iv. 14.) Our Lord had already preached in Lower
Galilee, at Nazareth, and Capernaum. This journey was to
Upper Galilee.

" And it came to pass, when He was in a certain city,
behold a man full of leprosy ; who, seeing Jesus, fell on his
face, and besought Him, saying, Lord, if Thou wilt, Thou
canst make me clean. And He put forth His hand, and
touched him, saying, I will ; be thou clean. And immediately the leprosy departed from him." (S. Luke v. 12-14 ;
S. Mark i. 40-45.)*

Leprosy was a disease the Israelites had brought with them
from Egypt ; it is the result of bad food, and neglect of
cleanliness. It is in the blood, which loses its usual character and colour. Probably the bondage of Egypt, with its

* S. Mark gives this miracle as occurring during the mission journey in
Galilee. S. Luke gives it after the miraculous draught. S. Matthew (viii. 2-4)
interrupts the order of events by the insertion of the teaching of Christ (v.-vii.),
which was the substance of what He preached on Galilee in this journey.

studied degradations and privations, and especially the work of the kiln under an Egyptian sun, tended to generate this disorder ; hence Manetho asserts that the Egyptians drove out the Israelites as infected with leprosy.

There were several hot springs near the Sea of Galilee, which were regarded as healthful in cases of leprosy, one of these, called Job's stove, was near Capernaum, but the most famous was the Spring of Miriam, near Tiberias.*

When Christ had healed the leper, "He straitly charged him, and forthwith sent him away ; and saith unto him, See thou say nothing to any man : but go thy way, shew thyself to the priest. and offer for thy cleansing those things which Moses commanded, for a testimony unto them." (S. Mark i. 43, 44.)   Till the man had been pronounced clean by the priest he was not re-admitted to associate with his fellow men.   He had not, for this purpose, to go to Jerusalem, but to shew himself to one of the priests who made the circuit of the land at fixed times, whose duty it was to take cognizance of the lepers and their condition. The offering for his healing was three lambs, and three tenth deals of flour, and a measure of oil.   (Levit xiv. 10.)†

Leprosy was regarded by the Jews as a figure of sin.   It was a creeping disease which affected the entire man, a

---

* The Rabbis said that "the rock that followed" the Israelites in the wilderness became fixed there, and the stream that gushed from it—hot—healed lepers.

† Otho lex. rabbin. s. v. Leprosus.

disease most hard to cure. Christ shows Himself by performing this miracle as the One Who is come to heal the world of sin, to drive out the poison which is corrupting the vital blood of mankind. Leprosy shut man out from the society of his fellows, and sin shuts man out from the society of angels. The leper was not allowed within the gates of a city, and sin excludes man from the Heavenly Jerusalem. There is but one source of healing for sin, and that is Christ. He took our nature upon Himself, to touch us, as He touched this leper, and by His contact with mankind He restores man, and restores Him by expelling sin from him. That is the true significance of the Holy Eucharist. Christ, before He left earth, instituted His great Sacrament as a means whereby He might still touch man, and touching him might cleanse, and heal, and strengthen, and restore him.

VIII.

The Sick of the Palsy.*

S. MATTHEW IX. 6.

"Arise, take up thy bed, and go unto thine house."

AFTER that our Lord had gone through Galilee preaching the Gospel of the Kingdom, and calling to repentance, "His name went throughout all Syria : and they brought unto Him all sick people that were taken with divers diseases and torments, and those which were possessed with devils, and those which were lunatic, and those that had the palsy; and He healed them." (S. Matt. iv. 24.) We have seen in our former lecture that the course our Lord took in His first missionary journey was through Upper Galilee, to the north-west, and then, probably, due east to Kadesh Barnea, thence He would proceed to the Jordan valley, where the river flows out of the marshy lake, the waters of Merom, and descend to Bethsaida, thus skirting Syria, and this would account for the fame of Him spreading in that direction. Thus He would have made a circular journey, returning by Bethsaida† to Caper-

---

* Suitable for the 19th Sunday after Trinity.

† Not the birthplace of Andrew, Peter, and Philip, which was on the west side of the lake. The name means the House of the Fish—a name given to any fishing village.

naum. This town lay three quarters of an hour distant from the lake at its upper end. It is now but a heap of ruin. Here it was, later, that the five thousand were fed. It was a small town, lately rebuilt by Philip the Tetrarch, and re-named Julias, after the daughter of the Emperor.

"And again," says S. Mark, "He entered into Capernaum after some days; and it was noised that He was in the house." S. Matthew says that "Jesus entered into a ship and passed over, and came into His own city." Accordingly He must have come down the Syrian side of the river to the Syrian coast of the lake, whence He took a boat and crossed the head of the lake to Capernaum. "And straightway," says S. Mark, "many were gathered together, insomuch that there was no room to receive them, no, not so much as about the door: and He preached the word unto them." S. Luke tells us that "there were Pharisees and doctors of the law sitting by, which were come out of every town of Galilee and Judæa, and Jerusalem."

The miracles He had wrought, and the novelty of His teaching had arrested the attention of the Rabbis and teachers of the law throughout all Palestine; and as formerly a deputation had been sent to John the Baptist to ask him his authority and teaching, so now, apparently, deputations waited on Him from Jerusalem, Tiberias, and elsewhere, Pharisees and lawyers of Judæa uniting with those of Galilee to hold an investigation into the conduct and doctrine of Jesus.

"And, behold, men brought in a bed a man which was taken with a palsy : and they sought means to bring him in, and to lay him before Him. And when they could not find by what way they might bring him in, because of the multitude, they went upon the house-top, and let him down through the tiling with his couch, into the midst before Jesus." (S. Luke v. 18, 19.) S. Mark only adds that the palsied man was " borne of four."

The roofs of the houses in Palestine were flat, with a balcony round them, and admission to the roof was obtained through a door in the roof of the upper chamber, or, sometimes, by means of a staircase from the outside. The houses in the town joined each other, and those who carried the sick man obtained access to the roof of the house where Jesus was, from the adjoining house.

In summer the people often sleep on their roofs, and the floor of this flat roof is consequently solid—of concrete, or of mud and straw, beaten hard. Palestinian houses have no special bedrooms ; sometimes part of the roof is covered with a tent, or thatch raised on posts. Towards the street are no windows, or only tiny openings, and light is obtained for the rooms from the court in the middle of the house, into which the windows open. There are

two explanations of the proceedings of the men who carried
the paralytic—either Christ was in the room, and the men
broke through the roof floor—which seems improbable—or
He was in the court in the middle, which is far more likely
to have been the case, as, by this means, a larger number
of hearers could be accommodated, and with greater comfort,
under the open heaven, than in a close and low chamber.

Round the roof, as a protection to those who are on it, a
balustrade of short tile pipes, set horizontally, was usually
erected. By this means a current of air passed over the
roof and cooled the sleepers.

Now those who bare the palsied man came on to the
roof from the adjoining house, and looking over into the
court-yard in the middle, saw Christ teaching there. They
pulled away "the tiling," that is, the balustrade of tile
pipes, which was breast-high, and so were able to let down
the sick man in the midst at the feet of Christ.

It was not uncommon to remove a corpse through the
roof instead of through the door.*

We read that king Ahaziah "fell down through a lattice
in his upper chamber," and it is probable that this upper
chamber was his lodging on the roof, and the lattice that
gave way was the balustrade that went round it. (2 Kings i. 2.)

Gemara, Moed Katon, f. 25. "When Rabbi Huna died, his body was
taken out of the house by the roof, because the coffin could not pass through
the narrow door."

The poor palsied man was utterly prostrate. He could not use his feet; he lay on the straw mat, which in the East serves as a bed, bereft of all power to move. But his faith must have been great; he must have endured much pain in being carried, and let down into the court by ropes. Great also was the faith of those who bare him. Probably his paralysis had affected his tongue. He could not speak, yet his very speechlessness was an appeal to Christ's mercy. His misery was a suppliant to the God of pity, more powerful than his tongue. The desire of the heart when addressed to God is at all times an effectual prayer. This was now the prayer of the poor man; hence it is not said that our Blessed Lord heard, but that He saw the faith of this man, and seeing it, He answered and rewarded it, though no vocal petition reached His ears.

He saw also the faith of the bearers, the friends of the sick man, who gave evidence of it by their acts, so that it was visible to man as well as to God.

"And Jesus, seeing their faith, said unto the sick of the palsy; Son, be of good cheer; thy sins be forgiven thee." It may be that the disease under which he laboured was the natural consequence of sinful indulgence, or, it may be, that by means of his sickness, a sense of sinfulness was aroused within the man, and that he recognized in his disease the punishment of his sins. In most other cases of healing we find our Lord first removing the bodily infirmity, and then that of the soul. The Jews regarded all sickness as the result of sin, and they even declared that the forgiveness of sin was a necessary preliminary to recovery of bodily health.* When Christ declared, "Thy sins be forgiven thee," it was not a mere declaration, like that of Nathan to David, that another had forgiven his sins. It was the voice of power putting away sin by His own almighty word; and so the Pharisees who heard Him understood Him. "And behold, certain of the scribes said within themselves, This man blasphemeth." They knew the declaration of God, "I, even I, am He that blotteth out thy transgressions" (Isaiah xliii. 25); they knew that to blot out sins was the prerogative of God, and they reasoned, "This man claims to forgive sins, therefore He is a blasphemer."

"And Jesus, knowing their thoughts, said, Wherefore think ye evil in your hearts? For whether is easier, to say, Thy sins be forgiven thee; or to say, Arise, and walk? But that ye may know that the Son of Man hath power on earth to forgive sins, (then saith He to the sick of the palsy,) Arise, take up thy bed, and go unto thine house. And he arose, and departed to his house. But when the multitude saw it, they marvelled, and glorified God, which had given such power unto men." So amazing

---

* Nedarim, f. 41. The Rabbi Chija, son of Abba, said, "No sick man is cured of his sickness, till all his sins have been remitted."

E

was the cure wrought in the face of the assembly, that the united deputations could say nothing against it, except take occasion at our Lord pronouncing absolution of sins, and even that they dared not utter aloud.

We can picture the whole scene. The narrow street without, between walls of basaltic black stone, crowded with people, who crush in at the door, and fill it. Those in the doorway look in through a short dark passage into the quadrangle in the middle, where, perhaps, grows a fig tree, and where the sun falls on the wall opposite. Those in the street have seen the advent of the palsied man. They have protested to the bearers that it is impossible for them to get through the crowd. Then they have seen how these men got admission next door, and went up on the roof. And now—a few minutes later, through the door into the street comes the paralytic, with his mat rolled up under his arm, and from above, the four bearers are leaning over the balustrade, calling to him, and uttering exclamations of delight and astonishment. The crowd divides, full of awe, and forms a lane down which the healed man walks. They are silent till he has passed, and then they burst forth into praise to God. There is a movement in the doorway. Forth come the Rabbis, the Scribes, and Pharisees, with faces clouded with annoyance, perplexed, harbouring bitter thoughts, yet afraid to give them utterance.

The remembrance of the claim to forgive sins made by

Christ must have produced a strong impression on them, for in the Talmud, the Jewish Rabbis declared that they refused to receive Him because He made this claim.*

Our Blessed Lord, in forgiving the sins of the soul, and in healing at the same time the body of the paralytic man, teaches us that He is the Lord and Redeemer of both body and soul. Paralysis is a figure of the state of the sinner, powerless through sin, more especially through indulgence in sensual lusts ; and the three instances in which Christ is recorded to have cured this disease typify three several stages in sin. He cured the servant lying sick of the palsy in his own house. He healed another who was lying impotent by the pool of Bethesda. And here He raises one lying helpless in his bed. He recovers from hidden sin at its initiation, and from sin notorious, and from that which has completely taken possession of man. We see the effect of sin on man—it paralyses him, it takes the power out of him to will and to do according to God's good pleasure, and we see also that with Christ alone is the power to recover man, and enable him to begin a new and healthy life.†

* Sanhed, f. 38, 2. Gloss.

† S. John does not give this miracle. He gives only samples of each sort of miracle—the miracle at Cana, the healing of the fever of the son of the Ruler, that of the crippled in the Temple, one multiplication of bread, one stilling of a storm, one opening of the eyes of the blind, one raising of the dead.

IX

The Miraculous Draught.*

S. LUKE V. 4.

"Launch out into the deep, and let down your nets for a draught."

WHILST our Blessed Lord was at Capernaum, His apostles, who were fishermen, continued their customary business, and so supported themselves and Him. When He called them on His arrival at Capernaum, it was to accompany Him on His missionary round in Upper Galilee. On His return home, they went back to the work of their avocation. "And it came to pass, that, as the people pressed upon Him to hear the word of God, He stood by the lake of Gennesaret, and saw two ships standing by the lake"—the Arabic version says "anchored to the shore." "But the fishermen were gone out of them, and were washing their nets; and He entered into one of the ships, which was Simon's, and prayed him that he would thrust out a little from the land. And He sat down, and taught the people out of the ship."

Zebedee seems to have been a well-to-do fisherman; he owned several boats. His family, and that of Alphæus,

---

* Suitable for the 5th Sunday after Trinity.

were partners in one fishing company. Perhaps there was a family connexion. These families of fishermen formed a kindly and peaceable society, extending by numerous ties of relationship throughout the head of the lake. Nothing of that which we call civilization, in the Greek and worldly sense, had reached them.

Tiberias was a heathen and Greek city, and was the habitual residence of Herod Antipas. We do not hear of our Lord having ever visited it, and preached there.

At the time of Christ there were 400 many-oared boats on the Sea of Gennesareth, and fishing was actively prosecuted in it. The lake is between 20 and 28 fathoms deep, but at the mouth of the Jordan it is only about 18 feet deep. A glassy line through the lake marks the current of the Jordan through it. The deepest part of the lake is between Tiberias and Magdala. The fish there are not so plentiful, owing to the hot springs which rise in the bottom of the lake. The numerous streams, and the shallows at the estuary of the Jordan invite the fish as spawning places, and the crystal water is alive with them at the head of the beautiful lake. They attract also multitudes of water birds. Beautiful shells are found in the streams, and the lake contains also a mussel like that which made Tyre famous by the production of its purple dye. Turkish misrule has devastated this beautiful land, and made of what, at the time of our Saviour, was the garden

of Palestine, a desolation. Now all the cities of Gennesareth are desolate, and only one small boat plies the waters
of the little inland sea.

The fishing was done for the most part by night; the
fishermen fixed torches to the sides of their boats, or held
them aloft, and the fish, attracted by the light, came about
the boats and were captured in the nets. S. Peter and his
companions must have thought of this when they saw the
multitude come crowding upon Christ. He, the Light of
the World, sat in the boat, where at night they fixed the
blazing torch, and as the fishes came thick about the flame,
so did now multitudes from every quarter come about the
True Light that lighteth every one that cometh into the
world. Sometimes, as they sat in their boats eating, they
had cast crumbs into the water, and at once from the blue
depths thousands of eager darting forms had appeared about
the food strewn for them. And now the giver of the Bread
of Life sits there, in the boat, and strews the word of God
among those who are hungering for instruction. " I will
make you to become fishers of men," Christ had said; and
the apostles saw what He meant, and how it was to be
fulfilled. They remembered the prophecy of Jeremiah,
" Behold, I will send for many fishers, saith the Lord, and
they shall fish them" (xvi. 16); and again, how Ezekiel had
said, in speaking of the restoration of Israel, that God
would send fishers who would gather into their nets men

"as the fish of the great sea, exceeding many" (xlvii. 10).

It is deserving of notice that Christ, although the Master recognised by the apostles, does not speak to Peter in words of command, but of courteous entreaty. " He prayed him that he would thrust out a little from the land ;" surely a lesson to us not to omit the little politenesses and refinements of life, even with those with whom we are on the most familiar terms.

It has been thought that the two boats were types of the Jewish and Christian Churches. The boat of Peter has been taken as the image of the Jewish nation and Church, and into this Christ entered, since He was Himself, according to the flesh, of the tribe of Judah, and was sent specially unto the lost sheep of the house of Israel, to whom salvation was first preached and offered, and through them to the Gentiles.*

" Now when He had left speaking, He said unto Simon, Launch out into the deep, and let down your nets for a draught. And Simon, answering, said unto Him, Master, we have toiled all the night, and have taken nothing : nevertheless at Thy word I will let down the net. And when they had this done, they inclosed a great multitude of fishes : and their net brake. And they beckoned unto

* One does not see, however, why S. Peter should have represented the Jewish Church, and SS. James and John the Gentile. A more plausible doctrine is that the two ships represent the Western and Eastern Churches.

their partners, which were in the other ship, that they should come and help them. And they came, and filled both the ships, so that they began to sink. When Simon Peter saw it, he fell down at Jesus' knees, saying, Depart from me; for I am a sinful man, O Lord. For he was astonished, and all that were with him, at the draught of the fishes which they had taken : and so was also James, and John, the sons of Zebedee, which were partners with Simon. And Jesus said unto Simon, Fear not; from henceforth thou shalt catch men."

Simon had toiled all night and taken nothing—a figure of all work done apart from Christ, much toil and no gain. But when we receive Him into the vessels of our hearts, then our work is blessed; whatsoever we do, we do all in His name, and in His power, and our work is fruitful.

How often, moreover, it is in the midst of that toil which we have undertaken as a duty of life, and when we are reduced to despondency and despair of success, that Christ interposes, and gives us more than we expect.

The fishers had toiled all the night ; they took this great multitude of fish in the same spot where they had been toiling without success, and they took it in the daytime. It is not when the times and circumstances seem to us most fitted for success that the work of God's Church is most prosperous, since His ways are not our ways. So may many a Christian labour through the night of this world, and seem to toil needlessly, but when the day of eternity shall dawn, it will be seen that his labour has not been in vain in the Lord.

It is deserving of observation that our Lord called these fishermen thrice. First, He made them His disciples at Jordan, when John the Baptist pointed Him out. Then, when He left Nazareth and came to Capernaum again, He called them once more, and that was to accompany Him on His mission circuit in Galilee; then to be hearers of His doctrine. Now comes a third call, and this time to complete renunciation of their trade. Now only did they "leave all and follow Him." First He enrolled them, then He partially detached them from their earthly business, now He completely disengages them from it.

"The net brake." That net is the Church; and the history of the Church is, alas! a history of the tearing of its meshes, and the breaking away of its fish. Heresy and schism have troubled the Church from the Apostolic period; and Christ in this miracle shewed that it would be so, lest we should be discouraged, but He also shewed the remedy for it—a remedy we have not sufficiently taken to heart.

When the net was torn, then Peter beckoned to his partners to help to receive the draught. And by this we are shown that the true remedy for heresy and schism is unity.

Sad it is that there should be so much separation among

the Apostolic Churches; that the Eastern Church, and the Church which claims to be founded by S. Peter, and our own English Church, should all be engaged in fishing on our own several accounts, with mangled nets, from which many escape, and in which only few are saved. When the Churches recognize the real cause of their failure, repent of their haughty and narrow isolation, and draw together, and call to each other to help, then, and then only, will they be filled to the bulwarks, so that they seem almost about to sink.   .

When Simon Peter saw the miracle, he fell down at the knees of our Lord, saying, "Depart from me, for I am a sinful man, O Lord." He recognised in the miraculous draught of fishes the exertion of a power greater than human. He had already been touched by seeing the miracle of healing wrought on his wife's mother, and now came this second miracle, touching himself, and he at once felt a conviction of his unworthiness. So should every recognition of divine power work in us a consciousness of our own shortcomings. That is no true conversion when man is puffed up with spiritual pride. S. Paul speaks of the effects of conversion in his Second Epistle to the Corinthians (vii. 9-11). "I rejoice that ye sorrowed to repentance: for ye were made sorry after a godly manner. For godly sorrow worketh repentance to salvation. For behold, this self-same thing, that ye sorrowed after a godly sort, what carefulness it wrought in you, yea, what cleansing of yourselves, yea, what indignation, yea, what fear, yea, what vehement desire, yea, what zeal, yea, what revenge."

The most certain evidence of the Spirit of God having touched man's heart is humility. S. Peter was crushed with the sense of his sinfulness; he was in a true state of grace, for he saw the contradiction which existed between his own living and the standard of holiness which God requires.

But, though Peter was full of humility at this time, this humble temper did not continue. Had it so done, he would never have given the assurance to Christ three years later, which called forth the warning of his Master that he would deny Him thrice. Consequently we may learn from S. Peter not to be content with paroxysms of penitence and humility, but to give to the mind a penitential tone, and so steep the soul in humility, that it may always fear its own weakness, and that so the whole of life may be a period of watchfulness and prayer against temptation.

X.

The Call of Levi.*

S. MATTHEW IX. 9.

"As Jesus passed forth from thence, He saw a man, named Matthew, sitting at the receipt of custom: and He saith unto him, Follow Me. And he arose and followed Him."

S. MARK adds something to his account of the call of Levi, given by S. Matthew. He says, " He went forth again "— that is, after the restoration of the man sick of the palsy— "by the seaside, and all the multitude resorted unto Him, and He taught them. And as He passed by, He saw Levi, the son of Alphæus, sitting at the receipt of custom." S. Luke adds nothing, but he gives the call of Matthew, whom he also names Levi, immediately after the miracle wrought on the paralytic.

Capernaum was on the main highway from Damascus to Tiberias and Jerusalem, and from Tyre and Sidon to Tiberias, and from Tyre to Bosra. The main road does not now reach the water's edge at Capernaum (Tell-Hum), but further down the lake at Tarichæa (Chân Minsch), but originally, in all probability, a road led from the Jordan

* Suitable for S. Matthew's Day.

valley, and the town of Julias, along the lake head, and the main road which crossed the Jordan at Jacob's Bridge to Joseph's Pit descended the little ravine past Chorazin to Capernaum, and thence followed the sea side to Magdala. A net of roads, in fact, met here, and indeed the whole of the East Galilæan trade passed through the place. The ships which came over the lake and unladed from Syria, paid dues here, as well as the goods brought by land. When duty was paid, the merchant received a card with a certificate from the customs house officer, without the production of which he might not dispose of his goods.

The officers of the customs, called publicans, were a despised race, not only in Palestine, but everywhere. The Greek poet, Aristophanes, says of a tax collector, that he was "an abyss, a whirlpool of plunder." Theocritus says that as lions and bears haunt mountains, seeking whom they may devour, so do publicans live in towns, preying on men.

In Judæa there was a poll-tax, a tything of the fruits of the earth, and a house duty. Duties were levied at harbours, and at the gates of cities, on all goods brought in.

The taxes were farmed out ; being put up to auction. The contract sum for Judæa, Samaria, and Phœnicia, was estimated at about 8,000 talents. An unscrupulous adventurer would bid double that sum, and would then go down to the province, and by violence and cruelty, like that of a Turkish collector nowadays, squeeze out a large margin of profit for

himself. Josephus, the nephew of the High Priest Onias,
paid 1,600 talents for the right to levy these taxes, and then
he took with him two thousand men-at-arms to Ascalon
which refused to pay, executed the magistrates, and wrung
a thousand talents out of the people. He did the same at
Scythopolis, and produced such a panic in the land that
no other city refused to pay the exorbitant sums he
demanded. Then he bribed the court of King Ptolemy
Euergetes, and succeeded in retaining the farming of the
taxes in his own hands for twenty-two years.

It may be well supposed that, with these unscrupulous
head farmers, the under-publicans were harsh and grasping.
Indeed, few men of character and self-respect would accept
a situation under them. The Jews regarded these collectors
with the abhorrence which they deserved. They were looked
upon as moral lepers, outcasts from society. so that it was not
lawful for a maiden to marry one of them, and they were
not allowed to give evidence in the purely Jewish courts,
as liars and false swearers by profession.* They were
classed with thieves and murderers.† Jews were not
allowed to receive money from them, to sell anything
to them, as the coin that had passed through their hands
was considered to have contracted a taint. ‡ If a Jew that
was married became a tax collector, his wife could obtain

---

* Sanhed. f. 25, 2 ; H. Demai, f. 23, 1,   † Nedarim, c. 3, 4.
‡ Bava Kama, f. 113, 1 ; Maimon. Gezela, c. 5.

a divorce from him on this ground. A tax gatherer was incapacitated from making a will.

It is certainly a striking thought that the Jewish race has sunk throughout the world, wherever dispersed, into what it most loathed in the time of its comparative well-being. Everywhere the national characteristic is that of the old publican—money-grabbing, unscrupulousness, usuriousness, so that the Jew has become the parasite of society, living on its vices—the social shark.

Matthew, or Levi, sat by the sea-side; he therefore took toll of the boats that came from the Syrian side of the lake. He is said to have been the son of Alphæus. Alphæus, or Cleopas, was the father of James and Jude, the cousins of our Lord; but probably the father of Levi was another Alphæus. If not, then we must suppose that Levi had been disowned by his family for taking up the base business of a publican. His call would mean also his reconciliation with his family; but we have not sufficient grounds to do more than think this possible. Cleopas, or Alphæus, was not an uncommon name. We meet with it again among the disciples of Jesus; it was that of one of the two who lived at Emmaus.

Money exercises a powerful fascination on man; especially does it seem to appeal to the worst passions in the Jew. A call to leave the lucrative business of publican was harder to obey than that which summoned from the fishing boats and nets.

The Lord came to the table where Matthew sat, and said, "Follow Me." Obedience was instantaneous. Conviction is sometimes sudden, and, if acted on, the life-vocation opens; grace acts on the soul. If, however, the call is put aside to a more convenient season, grace no longer acts, the call is not repeated.

The other evangelists, S. Mark and S. Luke, speak of the apostle by his other name—Levi. He himself, however, only makes use of that name by which he is known among the apostles of Christ—Matthew. Either he had two names, or, as is more likely, our Blessed Lord changed his name from Levi to Matthew when He called him from the receipt of custom, as He had before changed the name of another of His apostles from Simon to Peter; changing the name of those whose mode of life He changed when He bade them follow Him. S. Matthew, again, in the list which he gives of the twelve apostles, speaks of himself by this name, and adds that he was a publican, recording, as it would seem, in humiliation, his former disreputable vocation. In this call of S. Matthew we have a lively picture of God's call to us, and the way in which we should obey that call. God sees us, looks on us with the eye of His mercy, and by that look moves us to turn our eyes to Him. Then He calls us from the midst of our sins, from the occupations of the world, its cares and ambitions. He does so by various means, as the summons by which He called the apostles was not one, but

various—by various means and at various times. Lastly,
He enables us to rise up and tear ourselves from those pur-
suits which hinder our obedience, and keep us from God,
and as we strive to obey, He gives us strength to perform
what we perceive to be right, and desire to do.

When Saul chose his attendants, we read that if he
"saw any strong man, or any valiant man, he took him unto
him." (1 Sam. xiv. 36.) In this he followed the practice
of the world, and the dictates of human prudence. But
when Christ chose those who should follow Him, He,
whose kingdom is not of this world, called not the learned
and powerful to follow Him, but men of little repute, and
of lowly callings—the publican and the fishermen.

"And Levi made Him a great feast in his own house;
and there was a great company of publicans and others
that sat down with them." This is S. Luke's account;
it is deserving of notice that S. Matthew himself modestly
says nothing about his having entertained our Lord; he
merely says, "It came to pass, as Jesus sat at meat in
the house, behold, many publicans and sinners came and
sat down with Him and His disciples."

In the fulness of his grateful heart, the newly-called disciple of Christ made a feast for his new Master and fellow-
disciples—a sort of homely "paying his footing" when
admitted into their society—and he invited to it his fellow-
publicans; no others would associate with him. The term

F

"publicans and sinners" in our version is not quite correct,
it should be "publicans, sinners," that is, "sinful publicans." But there were others as well present, S. Luke
tells us, perhaps heathen.

The Jews and Egyptians, and, indeed, other peoples
were very scrupulous with whom they ate, much as are
the Hindoos to the present day. It will be remembered
that Joseph (Gen. xliii. 32) ate with his brethren apart,
and the Egyptians by themselves, for it was an abomination
to the latter to eat with Hebrews.* And so the old Tobias
(iv. 18), during the Assyrian captivity, exhorted his son not
to eat and drink with sinners. Christ, by sitting down to
table with these despised and excommunicate publicans,
and with heathen, broke through the caste rules, of which
separation at table was the most conspicuous symbol. He
shewed that this holding aloof from others, whether it
were national or individual, was contrary to the principles
of the Gospel, against the fundamental laws of His Church.
After that He had ascended, this was a tough matter for
His apostles to digest, and S. Peter had to be shewn the
vision of the great sheet let down from Heaven—a figure
of the Church—containing all manner of beasts, and be
given the monition, " What God hath cleansed that call
not thou common," before he, and the other apostles,

---

* Cf. also Porphyr. de abstin. iv. 7, " Ciborum et potuum extra Ægyptum
natorum non fas est gustare," and Herod. ii. 35, 41.

were prepared to extend the Church to those outside
the Jewish nation. When our Lord sent the Seventy
(S. Luke x. 7, 8) forth as forerunners of Himself, He was
obliged to lay upon them the obligation, "Into whatsoever
house ye enter, there remain, eating and drinking such
things as they give. And in whatsoever city ye enter,
and they receive you, eat such things as are set before you."
That is, make no distinctions about diet, as to what things
are common and unclean, and make no distinction of
persons, but eat with all alike. This was opposed to
Jewish Rabbinic maxims, for they ruled, " Thieves and
usurers are not to be associated with, even when they have
turned from their evil ways ; he who receives such into his
house, with him wisdom dwells not."* "Do not associate
with sinners, not even with good intentions of bringing them
to the knowledge of the Lord."† The Pharisees were not
allowed to touch any food prepared by a stranger, and now
at table sat together heathen and Jews, a Rabbi and Publicans. Well might the Pharisees and Scribes exclaim, " This
man receiveth sinners and eateth with them !" and ask
murmuringly of the disciples, " Why do ye eat and drink
with publicans and sinners ? " Then Jesus answered them,
" They that are whole need not a physician, but they that
are sick. I came not to call the righteous, but sinners to
repentance. Go ye, and learn what that meaneth ; I will

* Tanchuma, fol. 3, 2 ; Beracoth, f. 43, 2.   † Mechilta, f. 37, 2.

have mercy, and not sacrifice." Let all such as are weighed down with a sense of sin take comfort at these words. Christ came, as He declared, to call to repentance, and to pardon. He calls not the self-righteous, for they are so hardened by spiritual pride as not to receive His call. He calls not those who consider themselves whole, for they do not desire the interposition of a physician, but He says to such as are conscious of sin, to such as know their infirmities, " I will have mercy and not sacrifice. I am come to seek and to save such as were lost."

www.ingramcontent.com/pod-product-compliance
Lightning Source LLC
Chambersburg PA
CBHW022012050726
47499CB00007BA/2551